Poems From Kent Vol II
Edited by Michelle Afford

First published in Great Britain in 2007 by:
Young Writers
Remus House
Coltsfoot Drive
Peterborough
PE2 9JX
Telephone: 01733 890066
Website: www.youngwriters.co.uk

All Rights Reserved

© *Copyright Contributors 2007*

SB ISBN 978-1 84431 256 6

Foreword

Young Writers was established in 1991 and has been passionately devoted to the promotion of reading and writing in children and young adults ever since. The quest continues today. Young Writers remains as committed to the nurturing of poetic and literary talent as ever.

This year's Young Writers competition has proven as vibrant and dynamic as ever and we are delighted to present a showcase of the best poetry from across the UK and in some cases overseas. Each poem has been selected from a wealth of *Little Laureates* entries before ultimately being published in this, our sixteenth primary school poetry series.

Once again, we have been supremely impressed by the overall quality of the entries we have received. The imagination, energy and creativity which has gone into each young writer's entry made choosing the poems a challenging and often difficult but ultimately hugely rewarding task - the general high standard of the work submitted ensured this opportunity to bring their poetry to a larger appreciative audience.

We sincerely hope you are pleased with this final collection and that you will enjoy *Little Laureates Poems From Kent Vol II* for many years to come.

Contents

Barming Primary School

Edward Bryant (9)	1
Daisy Banfield (8)	2
Emily Baker (9)	3
Emma Heywood (9)	4
Jake Robinson (9)	5
André Tuffin-Inniss (9)	6
Karina Lappin (9)	7
James Bromley (9)	8
Daniel Reidy (9)	9
Billie-Jo Brooks-Coveney (9)	10
Alicia Stewart (9)	11
Alex Crampton (8)	12
Sam Tanner (9)	13
Erin Robinson (9)	14
Alex Affleck-Stewart (9)	15
Bethany Bevis (9)	16
Jack Bishop (9)	17
Kieran Buggs (9)	18
Florence Collins (9)	19
Jordan Duffill (9)	20
Natalie Featherstone (9)	21
Cliona Fletcher (9)	22
Adam Gordon (9)	23
Amy Gray (9)	24
Niamh Lund (8)	25
Luke Mallett (8)	26
Ruben Matthews (9)	27
Owen Robert McLeod (8)	28
Carla Louise Morgan (9)	29
Chloe Patey (9)	30
Emma Pearson (8)	31
Owain Pritchard (9)	32
Anna Katie Chapman (10)	33
Melissa Featherstone (10)	34
Georgia Humphries (11)	35
Alice Purcell (10)	36
Emily Jenkinson (11)	37
Alice Jenkinson (11)	38

Sean Hoyal (10)	39
Danny Ostridge (11)	40
John Haines (11)	41
Calum Elliott (10)	42
Tahmid Choudhury (11)	43
Francesca Flisher (11)	44
Kea Ward (10)	45
Christopher Hollands (11)	46
Ellie Potts (11)	47
Jack Richard Cooper (11)	48
James Owen (10)	49
George Wood (10)	50
Emma Boxall (10)	51
Alice Rogers (11)	52
Carolyn Rogers (11)	53
Dillon Panis (11)	54
Charlotte Wood (11)	55
George Atkinson (11)	56
Clara Matthews (11)	57
Robert Mount (11)	58
Sam Humbles (11)	59
Grace Clark (10)	60
Courtney Robinson (11)	61
Chloë Young (11)	62
Benjamin Town (10)	63
Fraser Cornwell (8)	64
Rachel Adams (8)	65
Emily Mortimer (8)	66
Alexandra Charlotte Hare (8)	67
Stacey Link (8)	68
Laura Featherstone (8)	69
Stefan Crowhurst (8)	70
Matthew Colley (8)	71
Tilly King (8)	72
Sam Gunner (7)	73
Arran Ostridge (8)	74
Hannah Morris (8)	75
Jade Hunt (8)	76
Ellie Livermore (7)	77
Aydan Janz (8)	78
Ellis Martyn Godfrey (7)	79
Elissa Jackson (8)	80

Rory Parker (8)   81
Katie Hyder (8)   82
Katie Alderson (8)   83
Noah Gorman (8)   84
Thomas Rollo (8)   85
Alisha Martyn (8)   86
Katie Town (8)   87
Heather Rose (8)   88
Beth-Ella Coleman (8)   89
Ben Cameron Morgan (8)   90
Francesca Sophie Syer-Thompson (8)   91
Michael Wall (7)   92
Jordan Benstead (8)   93
Jayden Reed (8)   94
Matthew Bolton (7)   95
Niamh Smith (7)   96
Simon Oakley (7)   97
Leah Young (8)   98
Jessica Harris (9)   99
Bethany White (9)   100
Megan D'Rozario (9)   101
Sophie Wahts (9)   102
Ashley Scott (8)   103
Jesse-Marie Havill (9)   104
Owen Bryan (9)   105
Callum Blackman (9)   106
Thomas Rumble (9)   107
Leon Stokes (8)   108
Charlie Boyce (11)   109
Elizabeth Ryan (11)   110
Joseph Crampton (11)   111
Daniel Judd (11)   112
Natasha Ives (10)   113
Emily Harris (11)   114
Katie Mills (7)   115
Taylor Fitzgerald (8)   116
Corryn Stacey Jordan (8)   117

Bredhurst CE Primary School

Marcus Wren & Zac (8)   118
Bradley Dowdall (9)   119

Joseph Hawkridge (9)	120
Zachary Burgess (8)	121
Kechi Onyekwere (8)	122
Shauna Sutton (9)	123
Emily Fleming (9)	124
Hannah Burgess (9)	125
James Kemsley (8)	126
Farrah Holland (9)	127
Aidan William Archer (9)	128
Lydia Walton (8) & Farrah Holland	129
Gary Treeby & Louis Rose (8)	130

Brookland CE Primary School

Amber Blake (10)	131
Amy Kolsteren (11)	132
Tonisha Leppard (10)	133
Jennifer Holmes (11)	134
Emma Jeffree (10)	135

Charlton CE Primary School

George John Snuggs (9)	136

East Court School for Dyslexia

Amy Davis	137
Max Ellison (11)	138
Grace Hardy (10)	139
Joseph Macari (10)	140
Oliver Kilbey (10)	141
Joe Catford (10)	142
George Herbert	143
Jonathan Sparkes	144
Dominic Wilkins (9)	145

Edenbridge Primary School

Danny Griggs (10)	146
Emma James (11)	147
James Bradford (10)	148
Amber Chatten (11)	149
Chelsea Broadbery (11)	150
Lauren Nazer (10)	151

Egerton CE Primary School

Isabel Cole (8)	152
Emmanuel Ephenus-Agostinho (8)	153
Alice Reed (8)	154
Lily Pevy (8)	155
Bradley Cain (9)	156
Jack Stubbins (8)	157
Emilia King (8)	158
Alisha Hameed (9)	159
Michael Carty (8)	160
Jake Hirvela (9)	161
Lauren Fox (8)	162
Rachel Pries (8)	163
Charlie Banks (8)	164
Harriet Heathcote (9)	165
Emily Gawler (9)	166
Eliza Wallis (8)	167
Katie Mills (9)	168
Ella Moore (8)	169
Erin Blackford (7)	170
Ella Woodcock (8)	171
Bill Hutt (9)	172
Joshua Simpson (8)	173
Sasha Gomez (9)	174
Amelia Simpson (8)	175
Alishia Mason (9)	176

Elliott Park School

Holly Plumb (10)	177
Grace Hale (9)	178
Toby Box (10)	179
Ellice Turner (9)	180
Harry Pierpoint (11)	181
Siân Ayling (10)	182
Tamara Layzell (11)	183
Freddie Pierpoint (9)	184
Matthew Edwards (10)	185
Tyler Pond-Field (11)	186
Bertie Francis (9)	187
Lacey Pavitt (9)	188
Billie Cook (11)	189

Hersden Community Primary School

Karl Edwards (11)	190
Ayesha Harris (10)	191

John Mayne CE Primary School

William Ruse (8)	192
Mark Sainsbury (8)	193
Amber-Rose Lockwood (7)	194
Sam Hackney (8)	195
Elliot Steward (8)	196
Jed Morgans (9)	197
Holly Palliser (9)	198
Thomas Agu Benson (8)	199
Emily Ruse (9)	200

The Poems

Anger

Anger is like a burning dragon
Anger is like the colour flaming red
Anger smells like burning smoke rising
Anger feels like your heart is burning
Anger reminds me of fear
Anger sounds like the world is burning.

Edward Bryant (9)
Barming Primary School

Love Poem

Love is red like romantic hearts,
Love looks like a candlelit dinner,
Love tastes of home-made cherry pie
And smells like the sweetest roses,
Love sounds like wedding bells
And reminds me of people getting on together,
Love feels like someone's touched my heart.

Daisy Banfield (8)
Barming Primary School

Sadness

Sadness is blue like the clear blue sky
It tastes like stale brown bread
Sadness smells like a damp street at night
It feels like black crows pecking inside you
It reminds me of loneliness
Sadness looks like lots of tears forming a clear blue lake
It sounds like a cute baby fox crying for its mum.

Emily Baker (9)
Barming Primary School

Love

Love smells like roses and makes you happy.
So when you look at things, it makes you want to pick them up.
The colour is like red and white mixed together.
Love reminds me of a bunch of flowers.
Love tastes like a romantic dinner.
Love sounds like soft drums.
Love looks like a red heart.
It feels like a romantic day.

Emma Heywood (9)
Barming Primary School

Fun

Fun looks like people having a pillow fight
Fun feels like people running
Fun sounds like people screaming with joy
Fun is a colour with light in it
Fun smells like good food
Fun tastes like sweets
Fun reminds me of the time I went to the zoo.

Jake Robinson (9)
Barming Primary School

Hate

Hate is red like blood flowing out of somebody,
Hate reminds me of a cruel bully,
Hate smells like the food you dislike the most,
Hate tastes of all your surroundings moulding into one
And going into your mouth,
Hate looks like a swarm of angry bees coming to sting you,
Hate sounds like the scream of 1000 people,
Hate feels like an explosion inside you.

André Tuffin-Inniss (9)
Barming Primary School

Happiness

Happiness sounds like tweeting birds,
The colour of happiness is a bright orange glowing in the black night,
Happiness looks like a ball of fire that has just been set alight,
Happiness tastes like mouth-watering sweets,
Happiness smells like fresh green grass being cut,
Happiness feels like you're strong and safe,
Happiness reminds me of the sun.

Karina Lappin (9)
Barming Primary School

Fear

Fear feels red in your heart,
It smells old and musty,
It feels rough like a jagged rock,
It tastes like salt,
It sounds like maracas shaking,
It looks pointed,
It reminds me of nightmares!

James Bromley (9)
Barming Primary School

Anger

The colour of anger is dark red,
Anger tastes sour,
Anger feels like you're burning up inside,
Anger sounds like the terrifying *bang* of a gun,
Anger looks like an empty graveyard
Where the bodies of lost souls live,
Anger smells like the tears of a helpless child,
Anger fills me with vengeance.

Daniel Reidy (9)
Barming Primary School

Love

Love is the colour of red, like an apple ready to eat.
Love looks like fire ready to cook on.
Love tastes like strawberry ice cream.
Love sounds like people crying in the playground.
Love smells like smoke.
Love feels like you're hot in the shimmering sun.
Love reminds me of me and my friends sitting around a fire.

Billie-Jo Brooks-Coveney (9)
Barming Primary School

Silence

Silence sounds like the sun shining down on the sand,
Silence is white like a room with no colour,
Silence looks like a blank page,
Silence smells like the sea drifting on to the sand,
Silence tastes like lettuce with no flavour,
Silence feels like no one is around you,
Silence reminds me of all of the great things
I have done.

Alicia Stewart (9)
Barming Primary School

Silence

Silence sounds like the super snow slowly meeting the ground,
Silence feels like a gentle breeze blowing on my cheeks,
Silence looks like chocolate melting in your delicate mouth,
Silence tastes like an orange's sweet juice,
Silence reminds me of an elegant bird swiftly swooping down,
Silence smells like the salty ocean crashing on the shore,
Silence is the pure colour blue,
Silence is great and I don't know what we'd do without it.

Alex Crampton (8)
Barming Primary School

Anger

Anger smells like smoke.
Anger is like the darkest red.
It sounds like someone yelling as loud as they can.
Anger smells like something rotten.
It reminds me of the First World War.
It looks like a furious boss at work.
Anger feels like a bee racing towards me.
It tastes like rotten biscuits.

Sam Tanner (9)
Barming Primary School

Hate

Hate feels like a flame of red fire blazing through your body
The sound of hate sounds like a mighty dragon
In an unforgivable fury
Hate smells like smoke from a burning building
The colour of hate is the colour of a witch's blood
Hate reminds me of a never-ending roller coaster ride
Of all the worst days of my life
Hate tastes like a glass of shredded chillies
Hate looks like the terrible sight of a deserted city
After a devastating hurricane.

Erin Robinson (9)
Barming Primary School

Anger

Anger is red like blood dripping out of a body.
It looks like a hurricane going around wrecking houses.
Anger sounds like people crying.
It feels like a raging skeleton.
Anger smells like a red devil.
It tastes like a pepper.

Alex Affleck-Stewart (9)
Barming Primary School

Laughter

Laughter is a colourful rainbow like people laughing and shouting.
Laughter looks like cheerful children playing about having
a chocolate ice cream on their jolly outing.
It sounds delightful, like youngsters having a fantastic time.
It feels like a lovely song with a rhyme.
It tastes like chewy strawberry sweets.
Laughter is red like someone bringing you some yummy treats.

Bethany Bevis (9)
Barming Primary School

Darkness

Darkness is black like evil power!
Darkness looks like a large monster.
Darkness sounds like lightning burning down a giant tree.
Darkness feels like extreme great power in my body.
Darkness smells like slimy, gooey, horrible, smelly sludge
going down the drain.
Darkness tastes like disgusting red blood.

Jack Bishop (9)
Barming Primary School

Happiness

Happiness is multicoloured like a beautiful rainbow floating in
the light blue sky.
It sounds like a bird getting ready to fly.
It smells like a red rose growing in a garden, and not like a pile
of foul-smelling clothes.
It feels like a cold bath after being in the burning hot sun.

Kieran Buggs (9)
Barming Primary School

Sadness

Sadness is blue like the deep blue sea lapping on the shore.
Sadness looks like teardrops dropping on the floor.
It feels like someone is hurting you without touching you.
It smells like damp wood rotting on a boat with no crew.
Sadness sounds like children who have been very bad.
Sadness tastes like tears coming from someone who is sad.

Florence Collins (9)
Barming Primary School

Fear

Fear reminds me of drowning in the middle of a huge lake.
Fear tastes like blood being drunk from a dead vampire.
Fear looks like complete blackness like being shut in a cupboard.
Fear sounds like a lady screaming in the middle of the night.
Fear feels like needles being pricked into you.

Jordan Duffill (9)
Barming Primary School

Love

Love is red like a rainbow filling the sky.
It sounds like birds whistling in the trees.
It feels like a warm feeling going through my body.
It smells like hot chocolate melting in my mouth.
It tastes like white wine being poured into my glass.

Natalie Featherstone (9)
Barming Primary School

Happiness

Happiness is bright yellow,
Happiness is the sun,
Happiness is like a brightly coloured rose blooming in spring,
It sounds like someone laughing loudly,
It feels like the softest pillow,
It tastes like sherbet lemons,
Happiness is like laugher and love,
Happiness reminds me of my family and friends.

Wherever happiness is, you will find laughter and love.
You'll never find fear or anger in a place of happiness.

Cliona Fletcher (9)
Barming Primary School

Fear

Fear is like a dark grey,
Fear is a hard stone that never breaks,
It is grey like slimy concrete being mixed,
It tastes like an extreme pain ready to emerge in sight of devils,
It sounds like an appalling feeling as if something is going to happen,
It feels like dreadfulness surrounding you in your heart,
It smells like distress and it loves to make agony appear.

Fear will stay in the world forever, so watch out!

Adam Gordon (9)
Barming Primary School

Darkness

Darkness is black like coal on a bright sizzling fire.
Darkness tastes like cola being drunk from a black bottle.
Darkness reminds me of being lost and terrified of not being found.
Darkness smells like polluted air all around you.
Darkness sounds like the wind howling in your ear.
Darkness feels very cold and frightening with no one around.
Darkness looks dull and scary like a monster appearing out of
black murky waters.

Amy Gray (9)
Barming Primary School

Happiness

Happiness is pink, like a flower in the breeze.
It looks like children full of happiness when they're having
the time of their lives.
It sounds like children laughing so loud you can listen to them
from miles and miles away.
It feels like you're having the time of your life.
It smells like sweets because they make you happy.
It tastes like a good time breezing through your hair.

Niamh Lund (8)
Barming Primary School

Love

Love is a clear crystal-blue stream.
Love sounds like a waterfall flowing down into the sea.
It looks like a sparkling blue crystal ball shimmering in the daylight.
Love feels like snow falling gently everywhere.
It smells like wonderful red wine racing straight towards the fresh air.
Love tastes like raspberries roasting in the refreshing sun.

Luke Mallett (8)
Barming Primary School

Love

Love is pink like a rose flowering in the meadows.
It sounds like a cool breeze flowing gently across the sky.
It smells like a never-ending aroma in the air.
It reminds me of an everlasting feeling where happiness never ends.
It looks like a heart that cannot be broken.
It tastes like chocolate melting slowly which you can feel trickling
down your throat.
It feels like a soft pillow at night.

Wherever love is, it is always with you.

Ruben Matthews (9)
Barming Primary School

Hunger

Hunger is brown like chocolate cake.
Hunger looks like yummy food you cannot reach.
Hunger sounds like the food is calling me.
It feels like it's making my stomach rumble.
Hunger tastes like Heaven.

Owen Robert McLeod (8)
Barming Primary School

Silence

Silence is golden like a bird singing beautifully in the trees.
It sounds like a cool breeze blowing the flowers gently.
It feels like a butterfly floating quietly onto your arm.
It smells like a red rose growing in the boiling hot sun.
It tastes like sparkling water fizzing in the bottle like it's going to burst.
It reminds me of a shimmering goldfish blowing tiny bubbles
in its bowl.

Carla Louise Morgan (9)
Barming Primary School

My Love Poem

Love is red like blood running through your body.
Love smells like roses blooming around the garden with honeybees
buzzing around them.
Love feels like a cold icicle running through your veins.
Love reminds me of fairies in the sky looking down on me.
And wherever there is love, you will find happiness all around you.

Chloe Patey (9)
Barming Primary School

Anger

Anger is red like a hot blazing fire spreading quickly.
Anger sounds like people screaming to get away from a building
falling down.
Anger smells like thick black smoke going into people's throats.
Anger feels like people running for their lives.
Anger tastes like a very poisonous drink.
Anger looks like a volcano erupting on a screaming village.

Emma Pearson (8)
Barming Primary School

Anger

Anger is *red* like a fiery flame burning inside you.
Anger is like loud, stormy lightning in the black sky.
It tastes like snow-white salt.
It sounds like crashing lightning in a wild storm.
It smells like bubbling sticky lava.

Owain Pritchard (9)
Barming Primary School

The Odeon

I can see the actors performing
I can smell the sweets that people are eating
I can touch the comfy chairs
I can hear people eating the sweet popcorn
I can taste the chocolate melting in my mouth
The film has ended
The lights come on
Everyone gets up
I think *it was great*
Next time I am going to bring my mate!

Anna Katie Chapman (10)
Barming Primary School

Nightmare

Tears rolled down my face
Who got me into this terrible state?
When I woke up I was in a horrible place
I saw worms on a plate!

Jaws snapping at me
What was I to do?
I could barely see
But I was sure it was only a shoe!

Why is a shoe snapping?
I was in a nasty dream
But all along it was tapping
Then I saw a beam.

That beam was really bright
It hurt my eyes
It was like a burning light
It was like a sunrise.

The sunrise made me feel warm
I tried to get out of bed
But instead I stood on a prawn
And laughed so much my face turned scarlet-red.

I could hear someone shouting my name
I sat there doubting
But nobody came.

Finally I woke up
It was only a dream
I sipped some water out of my cup
I tried to scream.

My mum nudged me lightly
I felt safe and sound
She hugged me tightly
It was great with Mum around.

Melissa Featherstone (10)
Barming Primary School

My Poem

Test going well until . . .
Oh, I don't understand this question,
My hand,
Not sure what to write,
Am I doing OK?

Turn the pages,
How many questions left?
Oh . . . loads more,
I'm getting worried,
What if it all goes wrong . . . ? But,
Am I doing OK?

I'll come back to that question,
I understand this question! Phew,
Next page now!
Am I doing OK?

Better hurry up,
Look around the room,
Is anyone else struggling?
Are they doing OK?

Test over now . . .
No going back,
Can't change anything,
I wish I'd answered that question
But . . . did I do OK?

Have to wait for results now . . .
When will they come . . . ?
What school am I going to?
. . . Results have come . . .

I didn't pass . . .
But I wonder something . . .
Did I do OK?

Will I appeal . . . ?
I'm going to Maplesden Noaks,
Will I do OK?

Georgia Humphries (11)
Barming Primary School

Holidays

Having fun in the sun,
Looking forward to it,
What will we do when the sky changes hue?
Have fond memories of bright barbecue flames on that night,
The suspense of my ride on the bike and down the slide,
And the water flumes and rapids that go, oh so fast,
With excitement as I get to the end,
On my way home, I'll post my postcards back,
All telling everybody the enjoyment that I have had,
With ten days to go, I can feel the excitement,
Building up, and up, and up inside me,
Like I'm going to explode like a can of shaken
Pop!

Alice Purcell (10)
Barming Primary School

The Performance!

When I walk down the street,
Shaking and trembling with fear,
Thinking *will I do it right*
Or will it be a disaster?

Here I am in the dressing room,
Trying to get my mind off things,
Trying not to think *will I do it right*
Or will it be a disaster?

I'm here on the side of the stage,
Waiting for my time to come,
Thinking *will I do it right*
Or will it be a disaster?

Here I am off the stage,
It wasn't scary at all,
I did it all right, no mistakes,
No way was it a disaster.

Emily Jenkinson (11)
Barming Primary School

The Competition

As the speaker spoke out loud,
I stepped into the ring,
Cheers were heard from the crowd,
So the music began to sing,
With my dog I was so proud.

As we sat on the ground,
The judges were looking around,
My family cheering us on,
I began to listen to the song.

Then my family was looking so happy,
Shouting, 'You've won, you've won!'
My puppy looked so happy,
Couldn't believe we had won.

Went up to the judge,
What was the prize?
Might be a piece of fudge,
But no, a collar for my dog, just the right size!

Alice Jenkinson (11)
Barming Primary School

Different Emotions

I'm bored
Always bored
As bored as watching paint dry
Just bored.

A dog barks
When a ghost's near
Am I scared?
Yes, I'm scared.

Someone's died,
How did they die?
I'm sad they died
Yes, I'm scared.

A child is born
A new life comes
In his mum's hands
He smiles happily.

I'm running away with sweat on my face
Being chased by a knight with a mace!
Is it fear?
Yes, it's fear!

Sean Hoyal (10)
Barming Primary School

Screamer

Everything is boring
Bored, bored, bored
The only thing that is fun is when Man U is scoring
They score, they score

My sister is screaming
Blood on the floor
And all over the door
I must be dreaming.

One minute I was watching football
Then there was fear
The screaming was from the hall
My dad dropped his beer.

Everyone scared
Panic through the house
We cared for her
Then there was silence, it was like a mouse.

I opened my eyes
It was a dream.

Danny Ostridge (11)
Barming Primary School

Hunting

The wolf is here
Hunting through the night
Stalking here and there
Menacing the moonlight
As it slowly retreats
Fear is in the air

The howl of the wolf
Kills any sound
The heart beating fast
As the wolf closes in
Its prey with fear in its breath
As it slowly retreats
Fear is in the air

Boom! The wolf's away like a shot
Racing through the trees
Boom! Fur slick with hot sweat
Its eyes blazing through the dark, *boom!*
As it slowly retreats
Fear is in the air
And the prey in its jaws.

John Haines (11)
Barming Primary School

The Men

Out of my head
The men stand staring
They are watching
Wherever you go
Whatever you do
They will be waiting
Waiting for the soul, yet to be repaid
One day they will find you
They need something
To help them
That something is you
If they want you, they will get you . . . !

Calum Elliott (10)
Barming Primary School

For The Day, Comes The Test

Feeling confused
Learning general knowledge
Also amused
Deciding your fate for college.

We know why we come to school
We come to learn
Not to act like a fool
Being a teacher's greatest concern

A year at nursery
Seven years at primary
Then comes sixth form and secondary
And finally university

Comes the day you dread
You do your best
The reason you should have listened to what the teacher said
For the day, comes the test.

Finally, it's completed
You can take a rest
Another test, 'be seated'
For the day, comes the test.

Your heart pounds against your ribs
Also your chest
Better not cheat or tell fibs
For the day, comes the test.

Tahmid Choudhury (11)
Barming Primary School

Excited

Excited
because it's
your birthday.
Excited
because of
presents.
Excited
because of
money.
Excited
because of
your party.
Excited because of the cake
And so excited you can't even sleep.
Excited because you're getting a dog.
Excited because you're getting in the car.
Excited because you're nearly there.

Francesca Flisher (11)
Barming Primary School

A Day At The Beach

Lying in your deckchair
Seagulls swooping past
High in the sky.

People are smiling
Children are laughing
Playing ball on the beach.

Swimming in the sea
Sunbathing on the sand
Everything is great.

Eating ice cream
Keeping cool
All on a day at the beach.

Kea Ward (10)
Barming Primary School

Scared

We wake up late
We are so annoyed
We're drifting in space,
While running in haste.
We're so far away,
We're out of time. 'Mayday!'

Teachers annoyed 'cause we're very late
My friends are going, 'You're dead, mate.'
I'm so late.

I'm now in detention
Oh why was I late?
The teacher's going to decide my *fate!*

Christopher Hollands (11)
Barming Primary School

Test Room

Test room,
Quiet and still,
Mark the question,
Right or wrong?

Test over now,
Another one tomorrow.

Test room,
Quiet and still,
Mark the question,
Right or wrong?

Test over now,
Has the testing stopped?
Find out,
Another test tomorrow.

Test room,
Quiet and still,
Mark the question,
Right or wrong?

All over now,
Can't go back,
Can't change the answer,
Missed out lots!

Will I pass?

Waiting,
I know I'm going to fail,
Waiting.

Go home,
Mum back now,
Open the letter slowly,
Scared to find out,
. . . *Passed!*

Go to the computer,

Anyone coming to my school?

Ellie Potts (11)
Barming Primary School

Animal Lovers

I had the strangest feeling,
Part of my body tingled,
I was so nervous.
I saw them,
I heard them,
They were wild,
Wild animals!

A monkey swinging happily,
A lion roaring loudly,
A gorilla fighting proudly in frustration,
An elephant squirting water whilst cooling down,
A baboon climbing easily,
Life with animals is worth it.

A snake slithering quickly, scared in danger,
A tortoise plodding along,
A hippo bathing,
Cubs playing nicely,
What a life to live!
I love animals.

Jack Richard Cooper (11)
Barming Primary School

The Day The Baby Came

I woke up on the day she came
I could not get back to sleep
It was so monotonous

Then came the sound - crying
The sound
My ears had found
That one sound!

Then I got scared the day the baby came
My mind suddenly flared
Ever so worried
On the day the baby came

And then my stepdad invited me in
And there was my newborn sister
Alive and living

And then I thought, *what if she died*?
I would probably commit suicide
On the day the baby came.

James Owen (10)
Barming Primary School

Cats

C reeping, creaking on the floorboards
A wfully scary, yellow eyes in the darkness
T rees swoop down, also having yellow eyes
S mashing everything outside, making a big mess!

George Wood (10)
Barming Primary School

Birthday

I feel happy when it's my birthday,
And I get it all my way,
Then there's a ring on the door,
It's my friends with presents galore.

I love it when we watch DVDs,
And play our PSPs,
After that the cake comes in,
And the wrapping paper goes in the bin.

I feel glad when it's my birthday,
Me and my friends get to play,
And we get to eat,
Lots of sweets.

It's my birthday
Hip hip hooray!

Emma Boxall (10)
Barming Primary School

Love And Hate

Hate is spiteful, a piercing sword,
Penetrating through joy, creating anger.
Hate means bloodshed, tears and wars,
Hate leaves scars,
Hate leaves gaping wounds.
Hate is oblivious to all good things -
Hate doesn't care, doesn't want to know.
Hate is the bully standing in the playground,
Hate is the terrorist, the vandal - not the ecologist.
Hate would rather take,
Hate would hate to give.

Love, on the other hand, is kind and gentle,
Caring and generous.
Love is the blossoming fruit that grows in all relationships.
Love means happiness, holidays and helpfulness.
Love is the servant, aiding the injured, helping the needy.
Love is the everlasting connection between two people.
Love will continue from beyond the grave.
Love is our heart beating, our life living for someone else.
Love isn't jealous; love isn't conceited;

Love loves the hateful,
Hate hates those who love.

Alice Rogers (11)
Barming Primary School

Senses

We were all created with senses,
We are able to hear, see, taste, touch and smell.
Some don't work and we need lenses,
They are all *vital!*

Hearing is a wonderful gift;
You can snuggle up and listen to secrets
Or hear Mum's voice while off you drift,
The comforting voice reassures your worries.

Sight - we can take it for granted:
Have you ever seen a breathtaking view
And were amazed at the planted trees, shrubs, flowers? -
What a lovely thing is nature!

Food, glorious food - oh how great
Cafés, bars, restaurants - places to nibble
How often do you clean your plate?
Taste - is it sweet, sour, savoury, salty?

Touch - what is it like, smooth or rough?
Is it bumpy, soft, hard or malleable?
Do you feel warm inside or duff?
Is it like running your fingers through the sand?

The sickly scent of pollen
Is sweet like a chocolate but sour as a lemon.
The musty smell of a woollen
Is horrible but important in our lives.

We were all created with senses,
We are able to hear, see, taste, touch and smell.
Some don't work and we need lenses
They are all *vital!*

Carolyn Rogers (11)
Barming Primary School

A Life Without People

A life without people
Is lonely and sad.
No one else to
Talk, listen or learn from.

Empty streets, just me and the road
Looking for someone.
Someone must be out there.
I'm on my own.

No one to love,
No one to hate.
I have no feelings,
They came too late.

They opened the heavens to me
And the Earth, but I have
Nothing in me,
Nothing but hurt.

They took me down,
Five bullets do hurt -
But I do not feel,
I feel nothing.

For I gave my love,
My life and my fate
To save them all,
All of the hate!

I bring them love,
I bring them happiness,
But I give them anger,
Anger and hate.

I am the bridge.
I carry your souls.

Dillon Panis (11)
Barming Primary School

Journey Underground

The call came in,
I felt sick.
I heard the scared voice,
Then a click.

I called for Dad,
He came down.
He could do nothing,
Nothing but frown.

We got in the car,
Drove down the street.
We got out and
Couldn't control our running feet.

The Germans were coming
Right above us.
People were escaping
By taking a bus.

We went underground
And met the others -
One sister, one mum
And two brothers.

Boom! Above us
Bang! A house.
We had to be quiet,
Quiet like a mouse.

Charlotte Wood (11)
Barming Primary School

The World

The Earth, praising the sun
For centuries and even longer.
Did the sun create the Big Bang?
Is the sun our creator?
One day we will find out,
Possibly some time later.

But there is God.
Is He the creator?
Apparently He created the sun, Earth, moon and us!

Ever since Man knocked on Earth's door,
We have killed it.
Nature is dying, the ice-cap is melting,
Gases are rising, the ozone isn't multiplying.
Humans are hitmen.
The Earth has written its death sentence.

Eventually the sun will part and start . . .
Start to burn everything in its sight,
Even Earth.
We can't stop that.
It will betray us, most definitely.

But that is ages away.
We can slow it down.
Save energy, recycle waste, use less water.
Let us have a future,
Let's wait.
That way we can make the sun late.

George Atkinson (11)
Barming Primary School

Emotions

Every time I get angry
My face goes red with rage.
Every time you make me happy,
My face brightens up with light.

Every time I have courage,
I feel as if I'm being cheered on.
Every time I'm feeling scared,
I feel as if I'm hiding.

Clara Matthews (11)
Barming Primary School

Emotions

Emotions are a part of life you cannot evade:
Happiness to sadness,
Anger to hate.
Emotions are a way of the world:
Love and joy,
Bravery and courage.

Anger makes you steam with rage
While sadness makes you droop in shame.
Love allows you to do crazy things
Although bravery makes you do amazing acts on impulse.

Emotions unleash your inner spirit
Which allows you to do things you thought impossible.
Every time you're alone, it feels like your emotions are escaping
But then, happiness emerges, showing you the light.

Robert Mount (11)
Barming Primary School

Why?

Why are people always sad?
I am not, as I am glad.
Why is everyone always happy,
When I am feeling like a baby's nappy?
How do people keep in touch
When I don't see my family much?
Why is it that I was scared
When they were not, so they just stared?
But why, to me, are they always mean,
Just because I'm small and lean?
Why?

Sam Humbles (11)
Barming Primary School

Hear

H ear the birds sing a song.
E ars listen to everyone and everything around me.
A s I fall asleep at night I hear dogs bark but not in sight.
R eady at last. I hear nothing, it's so quiet out there.

Grace Clark (10)
Barming Primary School

Different Emotions

It's good to be happy.
Happiness comes when people smile,
When it's a sunny day
Or when it's a weekend and you're having fun.

It's bad to be sad.
Sadness comes when people cry,
When it's a rainy day
Or when it's a working week and you are at school.

It's good to be calm.
Calmness comes when you are lying down,
Listening to peaceful music
Or when you're taking a nice stroll through the countryside.

It's bad to be angry.
Anger comes when you argue with someone,
When you fall out with a friend
Or when somebody breaks a precious thing.

Courtney Robinson (11)
Barming Primary School

Afraid

I'm afraid, I'm afraid of the spooky, spooky dark!
What's that? What's that?
Who's that? Who's that?
I'm afraid, I'm afraid.
I'm just a doormat, who's that?
I'm just a doormat.
Just tell me who's that?
I'm afraid of the spooky, spooky dark!
I hear a big bang,
Just tell me who's that?
I'm starting to feel terrified, I sniff feet.
People I hear, *bang, bounce,* what's that?
Who's that?
I see googly eyes. They're tearing me.
I wonder, *is it a bat?*

Chloë Young (11)
Barming Primary School

The Big Race

R ace is starting soon.
U nder pressure,
N early starting,
N ever slowing down.
 I n second place,
N ot so far away from first place -
G oing for gold!

Benjamin Town (10)
Barming Primary School

Happiness Is . . .

Happiness is blue like the pale blue sky.
Happiness reminds me of going to my first ever football match
at Upton Park.
Happiness tastes like lovely hot bangers and mash.
Happiness sounds like the calm countryside.
Happiness feels like a soft cuddly pillow.
Happiness smells like fresh clean air.

Fraser Cornwell (8)
Barming Primary School

Happiness Is . . .

Happiness smells like fresh perfume all around,
Happiness reminds me of all the special times in my life,
Happiness is like rosy-red pink,
Happiness feels like me hugging my teddy,
Happiness sounds like a bird singing in the morning,
Happiness tastes like chicken nuggets with chips.

Rachel Adams (8)
Barming Primary School

Happiness Is . . .

Happiness feels like a great big, white, fluffy cloud,
Happiness tastes like a great creamy chocolate cake,
Happiness smells like pink candyfloss,
Happiness sounds like birds in the trees singing sweetly,
Happiness is bright orange like a pumpkin on Hallowe'en,
Happiness reminds me of my hamster.

Emily Mortimer (8)
Barming Primary School

Happiness Is . . .

Happiness tastes like honey-roasted pork.
Happiness reminds me of fantastic, exciting times.
Happiness sounds like a tropical breeze from a desert island.
Happiness feels like I am relaxing in a shady place
on a sandy beach.
Happiness is gold like shimmering sunshine.
Happiness smells like the beautiful fresh air floating round the world.

Alexandra Charlotte Hare (8)
Barming Primary School

Happiness Is . . .

Happiness reminds me of juicy red strawberries dipped in chocolate.
Happiness feels like doing a super-high, amazing jump
on the trampoline.
Happiness sounds like lovely, tuneful and beautiful music.
Happiness smells like a cheese and tomato delicious pizza
cooking in the oven.
Happiness tastes like creamy brown chocolate.
Happiness is yellow like a hot, sunny sun.

Stacey Link (8)
Barming Primary School

Happiness Is . . .

Happiness sounds like children laughing in the park.
Happiness tastes like my favourite food, fish and chips.
Happiness reminds me of when my sister Kirstie was born.
Happiness feels like a soft, cuddly, blue-eyed bear.
Happiness is the colour of bright shiny silver.
Happiness smells like fresh clean air.

Laura Featherstone (8)
Barming Primary School

Happiness Is . . .

Happiness sounds like a tiny timid mouse nibbling cheese.
Happiness smells like freshly cut grass.
Happiness tastes like melted chocolate.
Happiness reminds me of my cat.
Happiness feels like a tiny soft kitten.
Happiness is the colour of the bright sun.

Stefan Crowhurst (8)
Barming Primary School

Happiness Is . . .

Happiness smells like pizza.
Happiness reminds me of fireworks.
Happiness tastes like cheese.
Happiness is yellow corn.
Happiness sounds like the roar of a lion.
Happiness feels like a slow breeze.

Matthew Colley (8)
Barming Primary School

Happiness Is . . .

Happiness tastes like melted, creamy, delicious chocolate.
Happiness sounds like little children laughing in the air.
Happiness reminds me of my best birthday.
Happiness feels like a soft, cuddly, furry, fluffy teddy.
Happiness smells like delicious roast potatoes.
Happiness is the colour of orange, flaming hot, boiling hot,
mega-hot molten lava.

Tilly King (8)
Barming Primary School

Happiness Is . . .

Happiness reminds me of my fun, happy 7th birthday.
Happiness tastes like some delicious chocolate cake.
Happiness smells like freshly picked strawberries.
Happiness sounds like a loud, noisy, long, rocking disco.
Happiness feels like soft, fluffy clouds.
Happiness is yellow like tasty vanilla ice cream.

Sam Gunner (7)
Barming Primary School

Happiness Is . . .

Happiness sounds like birds singing in the trees.
Happiness feels like when it is my birthday.
Happiness reminds me of chocolate cake.
Happiness is like the bright yellow sun.
Happiness smells like lots of wonderful flowers.
Happiness tastes like delicious sandwiches.

Arran Ostridge (8)
Barming Primary School

Happiness Is . . .

Happiness reminds me of a warm sun burning on me.
Happiness is like a warm red inside me.
Happiness smells like a crusty crisp piece of loaf just out of the oven.
Happiness tastes like a field full of juicy strawberries.
Happiness sounds like soft gentle music that has just gone by.
Happiness feels like a cool breeze blowing on your cheeks.

Hannah Morris (8)
Barming Primary School

Happiness Is . . .

Happiness smells like a rose that has just bloomed.
Happiness feels like a soft teddy bear.
Happiness tastes like a cold freezing ice cream sundae.
Happiness sounds like a sweet-singing robin.
Happiness is like the deep blue sea.
Happiness reminds me of when I first saw my pet dog Rocky.

Jade Hunt (8)
Barming Primary School

Happiness Is . . .

Happiness is like getting a new puppy.
Happiness smells like a chocolate bar.
Happiness tastes like spaghetti Bolognese.
Happiness sounds like laughter.
Happiness feels like a furry cushion.
Happiness reminds me of my snake going round my neck.

Ellie Livermore (7)
Barming Primary School

Happiness Is . . .

Happiness feels like Christmas
Happiness reminds me of strawberry milkshake
Happiness is like a bright blue sky
Happiness smells like crispy bacon cooking
Happiness tastes like a hot dog sausage
Happiness sounds like birds when you wake up.

Aydan Janz (8)
Barming Primary School

Happiness Is . . .

Happiness tastes like delicious chocolate.
Happiness reminds me of my birthday.
Happiness sounds like loud, crashing, thudding music.
Happiness smells like cheese and pineapple pizza.
Happiness feels like a furry, tiny, fluffy puppy.
Happiness is like the yellow bright sun.

Ellis Martyn Godfrey (7)
Barming Primary School

Happiness Is . . .

Happiness tastes like delicious melted chocolate in my mouth.
Happiness sounds like laughter on the seashore.
Happiness is as yellow as the golden sand.
Happiness feels like smooth silk.
Happiness smells as fresh as flowers.
Happiness reminds me of candyfloss being bought at the seaside.

Elissa Jackson   (8)
Barming Primary School

Happiness Is . . .

Happiness sounds like a *swoosh* from a butterfly's flutter.
Happiness smells like black shoe polish.
Happiness feels like candyfloss clouds.
Happiness tastes like melted chocolate oozing in your mouth.
Happiness reminds me of a snowy Christmas.
Happiness is like all the colours in the rainbow.

Rory Parker (8)
Barming Primary School]

Happiness Is . . .

Happiness feels like colourful butterflies gently resting on your arm
Happiness reminds me of popcorn at the pictures
Happiness smells like lovely hot meals
Happiness sounds like happy little children laughing
Happiness is as yellow as the bright middle of a daisy
Happiness tastes like colourful candy resting in your mouth.

Katie Hyder (8)
Barming Primary School

Happiness Is . . .

Happiness reminds me of my family and my good memories.
Happiness feels like dragonflies sitting on my nose.
Happiness sounds like a bird tweeting on a sunny day.
Happiness is like the colour of a lion's golden mane.
Happiness tastes like candyfloss melting in my mouth.
Happiness smells like sweetly scented lavender shining in the sun.

Katie Alderson (8)
Barming Primary School

Happiness Is . . .

Happiness is like the deep blue sea.
Happiness smells like tulips.
Happiness reminds me of the swimming pool.
Happiness feels like a cold snowflake melting in my hand.
Happiness tastes like lemonade.
Happiness sounds like the whistling wind.

Noah Gorman (8)
Barming Primary School

Happiness Is . . .

Happiness smells like lavender.
Happiness sounds like a waterfall.
Happiness tastes like the best chocolate melting in your mouth.
Happiness is like the lovely golden sun glittering in the sky.
Happiness reminds me of playing with my friends.
Happiness feels like warm water falling through your fingers.

Thomas Rollo (8)
Barming Primary School

Happiness Is . . .

Happiness reminds me of opening my presents,
Happiness smells like fresh-baked biscuits,
Happiness feels like a warm sunny day,
Happiness tastes like the colours green and blue,
Happiness sounds like guitar music.

Alisha Martyn (8)
Barming Primary School

Happiness Is . . .

Happiness is the colour of the bright yellow sun.
Happiness feels like my fluffy dog Sam.
Happiness sounds like the crunchy popcorn at the cinema.
Happiness tastes like the rich honey that bees make.
Happiness reminds me of when I got to play the cello.
Happiness smells like the beautiful lilies in the pond.

Katie Town (8)
Barming Primary School

Happiness Is . . .

Happiness is like golden dandelions.
Happiness feels like the gentle breeze on the beach.
Happiness smells like melting chocolate.
Happiness sounds like the gentle waves of the sea.
Happiness reminds me of going to the beach.
Happiness tastes like sweets melting in my mouth.

Heather Rose (8)
Barming Primary School

Happiness Is . . .

Happiness sounds like the gentle breeze.
Happiness tastes like beautiful chocolate melting in my mouth.
Happiness reminds me of my lovely holiday.
Happiness smells like the gorgeous little flowers.
Happiness feels like my mum cuddling me.
Happiness is like the gorgeous colour yellow.

Beth-Ella Coleman (8)
Barming Primary School

Happiness Is . . .

Happiness reminds me of when I play football with my friends.
Happiness smells like melted chocolate.
Happiness tastes like a very, very, jammy doughnut!
Happiness sounds like McFly singing a song.
Happiness feels like a calm river drifting through the world.
Happiness is as yellow as a sparkling sun shimmering on a beach.

Ben Cameron Morgan (8)
Barming Primary School

Happiness Is . . .

Happiness smells like beautiful and wonderful lilac flowers.
Happiness reminds me of my lovely family.
Happiness tastes like gorgeous chocolate ice cream.
Happiness feels like my mum cuddling me.
Happiness is the colour purple.

Francesca Sophie Syer-Thompson (8)
Barming Primary School

Happiness Is . . .

Happiness smells like outside in the garden.
Happiness sounds like waterfalls spluttering to the lower water.
Happiness reminds me of going to Taylor's
Happiness tastes like a yellow banana.
Happiness is the colour of the golden sun.

Michael Wall (7)
Barming Primary School

Happiness Is . . .

Happiness is like the colour of the blue sky swooping in.
Happiness is like chocolate melting in your mouth in the breeze.
Happiness reminds me of being in bed with my cuddly dog.
Happiness feels like me eating sweets.
Happiness sounds like a boulder crashing into Earth.
Happiness smells like the cakes I'm making.

Jordan Benstead (8)
Barming Primary School

Happiness Is . . .

Happiness feels like going down a waterslide.
Happiness sounds like me scoring a goal and everyone cheering.
Happiness tastes like chocolate melting in your mouth.
Happiness is the colour yellow.
Happiness reminds me of the yummiest chocolate world.
Happiness smells like the gentle breeze.

Jayden Reed (8)
Barming Primary School

Happiness Is . . .

Happiness feels like having fun at a party.
Happiness smells like pizza.
Happiness sounds like McFly.
Happiness is like dark blue.
Happiness tastes like Cadbury's chocolate.
Happiness reminds me of having fun with my friends.

Matthew Bolton (7)
Barming Primary School

Happiness Is . . .

Happiness sounds like my dog barking loudly.
Happiness is like the lilac of a salsify swaying in the deep breeze.
Happiness reminds me of meeting Mrs Moore and Miss Taylor.
Happiness tastes like popcorn.
Happiness feels like the sugar from candyfloss, making its way around
my mouth.

Niamh Smith (7)
Barming Primary School

Happiness Is . . .

Happiness tastes like chocolate.
Happiness reminds me of Thomas the Tank Engine.
Happiness is like the colour blue.
Happiness sounds like the ripples in water.
Happiness feels like people in the park.
Happiness smells like melting chocolate.

Simon Oakley (7)
Barming Primary School

Happiness Is . . .

Happiness reminds me of the ice cream van,
Happiness smells like fresh-baked biscuits,
Happiness feels like a cosy bed,
Happiness tastes like fresh warm bread,
Happiness is like the colour blue,
Happiness sounds like wind blowing through the trees.

Leah Young (8)
Barming Primary School

Fun

Fun makes you happy like a party is happening
Fun is like a big yellow sun going by
Fun tastes like a big ripe strawberry ready to burst
Fun sounds like happy children playing on a hot summer's day
Fun is the colour of a bright sun on a summer's day
Fun looks like a big yellow balloon ready to fly away
never to be seen again.

Jessica Harris (9)
Barming Primary School

A Poem Of Happiness

Happiness is like the sweet smell of bright scented flowers
Happiness smells like delicious melted chocolate
Happiness looks like people's fantastic friendships
Happiness tastes like a lovely Sunday dinner
Happiness is yellow like the hot shining sun
Happiness sounds like laughing children running around
Happiness feels like a warm cosy home.

Bethany White (9)
Barming Primary School

Love Poem

Love smells like the sweet smell of bright red roses
Love looks like your mum and dad as they kiss you goodnight
Love is the colour of pink little bunnies' ears popping up from the
holes in the ground
Love tastes like melted chocolate
Love reminds me of happy times we have as a family
Love feels like warm cuddles from your mum and dad.

Megan D'Rozario (9)
Barming Primary School

Love Poem

Love is like pink roses
And smells like the romantic smell of sweet flowers.
Love tastes like mouth-watering raspberries with delicious strawberries.
Love reminds me of the lovely different coloured flowers.
Love feels happy, joyful and warm inside.
Love is a magnificent sound.

Sophie Wahts (9)
Barming Primary School

Anger

Anger looks like dark bulgy eyes
It feels like you are in disguise
It sounds like something is behind you
Anger is the colour of black and red
It tastes like something you will throw up from
It smells like the smelliest thing in the whole entire world
It reminds me of something I hate.

Ashley Scott (8)
Barming Primary School

Laughter

Laughter is orange like a ginger purring cat
Laughter sounds like happiness to all children
Laughter looks like a big, comforting hug from your mother
Laughter tastes like sweet cherries in the middle of summer
Laughter smells like a small bonfire with roasting marshmallows over it
Laughter feels like a pleasant cool breeze of fresh air
Laughter reminds me of times when I have been in a snug house.

Jesse-Marie Havill (9)
Barming Primary School

Jealousy

Jealousy is like light red
Jealousy feels like ice melting in your heart
Jealousy reminds me of being scared
And being let down
It looks like it's raining on an empty street
Jealousy sounds like drums
Jealousy smells like rotted wood
It tastes like warts and scabs.

Owen Bryan (9)
Barming Primary School

Darkness

Darkness is black like the black sky at night.
It looks like when you are in space
And another name for bad.
It sounds like silence.
It feels like rich brown earth.
It smells like a damp slippery floor.
It tastes like treacle in a dish which has cooled.

Callum Blackman (9)
Barming Primary School

Anger

Anger is red like blood dripping out of a dead animal.
Anger looks like you're about to explode in a second.
Anger tastes like cherries just about to be eaten.
It smells like lava just about to burst out of a volcano.
Anger sounds like a trumpet just about to blow a very loud sound.
Anger feels as if I'm about to burst in a second.
Anger reminds me of a volcano just about to erupt.

Thomas Rumble (9)
Barming Primary School

Fun

Fun is green like new leaves.
It looks like a baby bird.
It sounds like children playing and running.
It feels like jumping around.
It smells like fresh air.
It tastes like ice cream.

Leon Stokes (8)
Barming Primary School

Fear Poem

When a wolf howls
A tiger prowls
It brings fear
And you know it's near.

It is dark
Something beating fast
It must be the heart
It brings fear
And you know it's near.

Someone listens with their ear
They hear footsteps growing near
It brings fear
And it is near.

Something does appear
That he most fears
It brings fear
And it is near.

He runs away
Into the new day
It brings fear
And you know it's here.

Charlie Boyce (11)
Barming Primary School

Getting Wet

G lory to water
E verlasting fun
T idal wave
T idal wave
I n the boat
N ow very wet
G etting soaked from head to toe.

W alls of water hitting your face
E verlasting joy at the moment
T horoughly loving it!

Elizabeth Ryan (11)
Barming Primary School

My First Dive

Standing,
Waiting,
Deep breaths.
I'm shaking,
Everyone's looking.
I'm nervous,
I want to get down.
No!
I've *got* to do this.
I look down,
The water, full of sequins,
Is waiting,
Waiting for me.
I've *got* to do this.
I close my eyes,
I jump,
Like a flying dolphin
Soaring through the air,
I *am* doing this.
Splash!
I *did* it.
I'm on top of the world!

Joseph Crampton (11)
Barming Primary School

The Really Weird Dream

I tried, I tried,
I was almost there.
I cried, I cried,
It wasn't fair.

I begged, I begged,
For dear life.
They denied, they denied,
They pulled out a knife.

I called, I called,
For more help.
They came, they came,
I let out a 'yelp'!

I was saved, I was saved,
I felt so glad.
This dream, this dream,
Was rather mad!

But still, I still,
Thought I was dead.
I wasn't, I wasn't . . .

I woke up in bed!

Daniel Judd (11)
Barming Primary School

Summer

Summer, summer,
Summer is coming,
Everyone is going to have fun
In the sun.
Playing and saying 'I'm hot' a lot.

I'm not glum, I love plums,
But only some.
I am having so much fun
In the sun.
Keeping cool in the pool,
All day long,
So sing a song.
I'm having so much fun
In the sun!

Natasha Ives (10)
Barming Primary School

Scaredy-Cat

I'm scared, I'm scared.
No one's there, no one's there.
Who's that? Who's that?
It's just a bag, it's just a bat.
Ahhhh . . .
No, don't scream, don't scream!
I'm only a cat, I'm only a cat,
A big scaredy-cat!

Emily Harris (11)
Barming Primary School

Happiness Is . . .

Happiness tastes like nice sweet strawberries.
Happiness sounds like singing birds singing in the breeze.
Happiness feels like nice soft kittens' new fur.
Happiness reminds me of my favourite rabbit.
Happiness is like a bright, colourful rainbow.
Happiness smells like flower-smelling perfume.

Katie Mills (7)
Barming Primary School

Happiness Is . . .

Happiness reminds me of a happy time in my life like my birthday!
Happiness smells like red roses in a lovely garden!
Happiness feels like a happy time in my life.
Happiness is the colour of bright, lovely, wonderful,
marvellous sunlight.
Happiness sounds like birds chirping in the fascinating trees in the
lovely summer!
Happiness tastes like ice cream with every topping in the world
With a lollipop on the side, with Coke for a drink and a chocolate Flake
With a warm bacon sandwich!

Taylor Fitzgerald (8)
Barming Primary School

Happiness Is . . .

Happiness sounds like a large waterfall.
Happiness reminds me of when I went out with my family.
Happiness tastes like pasta bake.
Happiness feels like when my mum strokes my hair.
Happiness smells like the beautiful flowers.
Happiness is like a beautiful rainbow.

Corryn Stacey Jordan (8)
Barming Primary School

The Magic Box

(Based on 'Magic Box' by Kit Wright)

I will put in my box . . .

A glittery colourful rainbow
A walking plant pot
A dancing apple with spirits in it.

I will put in my box . . .

A boomerang that never comes back
A talking, terrifying TV
A cup that when you touch it, smashes.

I will put in my box . . .

A dog that fetches stuff then never brings anything back
A cat with elephant ears
A dog that poos on every patch of the floor.

My box opens by a shoot-out card.
My box is made out of silver and gold stars that glitter at night.

Marcus Wren & Zac (8)
Bredhurst CE Primary School

The Magic Box

(Based on 'Magic Box' by Kit Wright)

I will put in the box . . .

A pink 82-ton tank that walks
A four-ton elephant that eats people
A double-sized burger from Mars.

I will put in the box . . .

A four-metre long bacon burger from Jupiter
A kangaroo that jumps 100 metres in the air
A king cobra that could eat Mars in one.

I will put in the box . . .

A 50,000lb mouse that is the size of the M25
A sofa that comes alive from DFS
A red shark that is 2½ miles long.

I will put in the box . . .

A man-eating house that will eat you.
A snail that is 1cm long and smells like poo
A gold star from Starland.

The box will be styled from . . .
Frozen Coke which never melts
The hinges will be made of eyeballs
And there will be adders on the shiny gold lid.

Bradley Dowdall (9)
Bredhurst CE Primary School

My Magic Box

(Based on 'Magic Box' by Kit Wright)

I will put in my box . . .

A dangerous red unicorn
A turquoise tap-dancing tarantula
A famished, starving, blue T-rex.

I will put in my box . . .

Twelve shreds of David Beckham's hair
A dream cricket set
Jonny Wilkinson's white rugby shirt.

I will put in my box . . .

Horrid Henry's old trainers
Harry Potter's white wand
Jeremy Clarkson's Ferrari.

Joseph Hawkridge (9)
Bredhurst CE Primary School

The Magic Box

(Based on 'Magic Box' by Kit Wright)

I will put in the magic box . . .

A walking multicoloured plant,
A talking TV,
A boomerang that never comes back.

I will put in the magic box . . .

A rising, radiant rainbow,
A dog that fetches but never brings the ball back,
Santa's rumbling fat tummy.

I will put in the magic box . . .

A dancing purple apple,
A cup that when you touch it, smashes a man with 20 legs.

My box is fashioned from green and blue crystals,
To open it you must put a Doctor Who card in a slot.

In my box I will go go-kart racing around a grey, gravel track,
Fight a dragon with a sword,
Swim with sharks in the Pacific Ocean.

Zachary Burgess (8)
Bredhurst CE Primary School

Magic Box

(Based on 'Magic Box' by Kit Wright)

I will put in the box . . .

The first cake to cost £10,000,
The first sparkling star I saw at night,
The most exciting day of my life.

I will put in the box . . .

A tiny, six-legged spider who says hello,
A flash of sunlight at the time of the moon,
A vegetarian dinosaur that is scared of old people.

I will put in the box . . .

An evil mouse who picks up elephants,
A sprinkle of fairy dust that makes me growl,
My ancient uncle who never smiles.

My box is fashioned from icy diamonds found in the North Pole.
The hinges are made of toenails taken from the American dragon,
But of course the lid and the bottom of the box are covered with
the notes Diana Ross sang.

I shall zoom across the big wide world
And meet new friends that I have never seen before.
I may even go to space and see some aliens from Mars.

Kechi Onyekwere (8)
Bredhurst CE Primary School

The Magic Box

(Based on 'Magic Box' by Kit Wright)

I will put in my box . . .

Flying fairies flittering quickly,
Sparkling pandas in India,
A lizard with a green long tail.

I will put in my box . . .

A cake with a millipede in it,
An old wrinkly photo of my Victorian family,
A golden wig from my mum.

My box is fashioned from a purple steel box,
With gold stars on the lid,
The hinges are carrot-gold,
There are magic eyelashes everywhere
And secrets in the corners.

I shall ice-skate with my box as shoes on the desert
Then skate to the sun.

Shauna Sutton (9)
Bredhurst CE Primary School

The Magic Box

(Based on 'Magic Box' by Kit Wright)

I will put in my magic box . . .

A splash of a purple dolphin swimming in the sea.
A blink of a Chinese dragon wiggling through the street.
A bushy tail of a squeaking cat chasing a mouse.

I will put in my magic box . . .

Bouncing, boring, green spaghetti on my plate ready to eat.
The spring of a green rabbit eating grass
And a blue hopping pig eating some food.

I will put in my magic box . . .

A walking talking apple ready to eat.
A munching violet worm singing pop songs.
A slimy red snail eating cabbage and dancing under the moon.

Emily Fleming (9)
Bredhurst CE Primary School

The Magic Box

(Based on 'Magic Box' by Kit Wright)

I will put in the box . . .

A diving purple dolphin splashing through the waves,
A handstanding green rabbit running round the sparkling pavement,
A hair and coleslaw chuckling sandwich.

I will put in the box . . .

A blue hopping pig going round and round in circles,
A brown bowl of chatting black sweets trying to get out of a layer
of ketchup,
A miaowing field mouse chatting to a cat.

I will put in the box . . .
A flying red snail singing in the rain,
A green odious cheetah shuffling on his bottom,
A violet worm munching on a bird while choking in the process.

I will put in the box . . .

A blue, walking, talking apple,
A black Chinese dragon breathing air,
A green springing piece of spaghetti.

My box is fashioned out of yellow ice,
With purple shiny leaves for the lid
And horns from an elephant and eyelids from a kangaroo.

Hannah Burgess (9)
Bredhurst CE Primary School

The Magic Box

(Based on 'Magic Box' by Kit Wright)

I will put in my box . . .
A piece of Beckham's hair.
I will put in my box . . .
A huge, juicy, fat, silver apple.
I will put in my box . . .
A unicorn's head and legs.

I will put in my box . . .
A little model of Michael Owen.
I will put in my box . . .
£1,000 so I can buy a Hummer.

I will put in my box . . .

James Kemsley (8)
Bredhurst CE Primary School

The Magic Box

(Based on 'Magic Box' by Kit Wright)

I will put in the box . . .

A kiss from a relative who died,
A famished great white shark playing with people,
The first smile from a grumpy boy.

I will put in the box . . .

An old rusty sapphire created by a mine,
A sunbeam from a multicoloured sun,
A yellow pig flying over the moon.

I will put in the box . . .

A red orca from the Southern Ocean,
A dolphin flying in outer space,
A flying pearl chirping like a bird.

I will put in the box . . .

A flying cow singing over mountains,
A baby-blue panther purring and squealing
And a cold chill from Antarctica, swishing and swirling.

Farrah Holland (9)
Bredhurst CE Primary School

The Magic Box

(Based on 'Magic Box' by Kit Wright)

I will put in the box . . .

My gold, glowing, glorious ball
A rock with an avalanche on its front
My fantastic, fun football socks

I will put in the box . . .

A silver moon that shines on my blue silky quilt
One of Henry's best goals
A bullet from a golden gun

I will put in the box . . .

A first ever toy
The first word I said
The shining, slender, sunny sun

My box is fashioned from
A dinosaur's toenail
A piece of see-through gold
And a fin of a shark

I shall surf in my box
On the great waves of Hawaii
Then catch fish on the beach
And have fish and chips for lunch.

Aidan William Archer (9)
Bredhurst CE Primary School

The Magic Box

(Based on 'Magic Box' by Kit Wright)

I will put in the box . . .

A glittering fairy winking,
A baby pig flying over the moon,
A kiss from a relative.

I will put in the box . . .

The first dolphin out in space,
A sardine eating a whale.

I will put in the box . . .

An Indian flying on a muddy donkey,
A really lovely smile from a grumpy boy,
A horrible animal and its prey.

I will put in the box . . .

A flying, snapping clam,
A nice Arctic breeze,
A tan from an unusual sun,
An ant eating a hippopotamus.

Lydia Walton (8) & Farrah Holland
Bredhurst CE Primary School

The Magic Box

(Based on 'Magic Box' by Kit Wright)

I will put in the box . . .

A vegetarian lion who
Is scared of cats
And wouldn't say boo to a goose.

I will put in the box . . .

An evil eagle who picks
Up elephants at 400 miles per hour
And drops them suddenly in Australia.

I will put in the box . . .

My favourite food which is KFC and McDonald's
So the person who delivers it has a car with cheetah legs
Instead of wheels.

My box is made out of . . .
Metal with crystals decorating all over the box.

Gary Treeby & Louis Rose (8)
Bredhurst CE Primary School

The Midnight Sky

Have you seen the moon shimmer in the sky?
Have you seen the stars twinkling up high?
The midnight sky will glisten in the dark
With its gentle breeze playing in the park.

A black blanket takes charge of the sky
As the moonlit stars watch the day go by.
The night-time animals come out to play
Before the dark night fades away.

As the moon and stars start to sleep
They know the midnight sky is theirs to keep.
They will appear in the night sky again
And will welcome you as their friend.

Amber Blake (10)
Brookland CE Primary School

The Teacher's Prayer

Dear Lord,

Please let the store cupboard be locked, bolted and secured
before I go back to school.
I don't want any 'accidents'.
And Lord, let the children understand curriculum weight
So I do not have to waste time explaining it later.
Let the year 6s stop putting thumb tacks on my chair.

Amen.

Amy Kolsteren (11)
Brookland CE Primary School

A Day At The Beach

Sand, sand under the sea
Gently swishing against me
Children playing with the sand
As their parents are giving commands
Sunbeds and shade, that's what you need
When the parents are starting to feed
Time to get out now, don't you think?
In a minute you'll be starting to sink
On the way home, I start to sleep
As the car is going *beep! Beep!*

Tonisha Leppard (10)
Brookland CE Primary School

My Best Friend

E verything she does is cool,
M an, she is always in that pool,
M any things we do are fun,
A lways we play in the red-hot sun!

Jennifer Holmes (11)
Brookland CE Primary School

I Wish I Was A Teacher

A teacher I wish to be
Teaching children their ABC.
I will teach them to count too
Hopefully to twenty-two!

At break times I will sit in the staff room
'Cause outside is the hall of doom!
I will hold my mug of scorching hot tea
Even though it makes me pee!

Big children, small children, children going up in flares,
There are children everywhere!

Emma Jeffree (10)
Brookland CE Primary School

River

River going, also flowing, on a summer's day,
Water flushes, really gushes, down the river lane.
Water gushes, swirling on the rocks below.

Winter comes, turning slushy water into brown,
The water freezes and sadly we have to go!

George John Snuggs (9)
Charlton CE Primary School

Pink

Pink is my favourite colour
It's painted all over my room
So whenever I go in there
It cheers me from my gloom!
The flamingos all went pink
Because of what they eat
But if they didn't eat that
They wouldn't have any feet!

Amy Davis
East Court School for Dyslexia

Green

G reen grass is green, apples are too. Walls covered in moss
R eeds by the pond are swaying
E ver so green are the limes and mangoes
E very green snake is scary
N ew grass and green leaves start to come out in spring.

Max Ellison (11)
East Court School for Dyslexia

Through My Telescope

I see a red juicy cherry
Then a mouse, a small field mouse
It's shiny, black and brown, cute and sweet
I zoom out. I see a sweet-smelling cornfield, gold and yellow
I see green and brown trees in the countryside
Fresh air, *mmmm!*
Then the shape of England
I smell salt. I see blue and green
It's the sea, waves crashing together
The whole world is green and blue
I see the world rotating with a black space all around it
Twinkling stars and shining moon brighten up the world.

Grace Hardy (10)
East Court School for Dyslexia

Telescope Poem

Black as night
volcanic rock
a black mountain of heavy, lumpy rock
a mass of lava leaping out of the top of the mountain
a red-hot volcano
a village being slain by the volcanic ash
Italy in flames
the sea tinged in fear, death and sorrow
within the unsuspecting world
the world spinning in space
with a burning black hole
the rest of the universe calm
as if it never happened.

Joseph Macari (10)
East Court School for Dyslexia

Sunset Over The Sea

Yellow
red, orange
sun, muddy waves
relaxing, tranquil, calm, glowing
stones, pebbles, still blue waves
sun setting, reflecting ripples flowing away
round sun, long, thin, watery reflection shining
speedboat, white wake behind it
bright blue yacht sailing.

Oliver Kilbey (10)
East Court School for Dyslexia

The Noble Tiger

Orange
transparent water
threatening but still
staring, emotionless, amber eyes
the white stripes of death
black dangerous markings with ancient beauty
the noble tiger leaps for the kill.

Joe Catford (10)
East Court School for Dyslexia

The Satellite

Tall metal pole
Hard black ball attached to the top
A sort of dish at the bottom
In a green grassy field
Nearby, a deserted old village
Motorway circling around it
Dover, ships going to France
Spain, the Straits of Gibraltar
Across from the massive continent Africa
The round curves of the Earth appear.

George Herbert
East Court School for Dyslexia

The Sea

Grey
Jagged rocks
A lively place
Fierce white, spraying water
Waves smashing against the cliffs
The outcrop battling against the waves
The cliff crumbling while the waves hit
Crazy currents making the water wave and bubble
A loud thundering sound which echoes in your ears
The powerful waves are smashing and crashing into the cliff.

Jonathan Sparkes
East Court School for Dyslexia

Chinese Garden Painting

Glowing
turquoise, peach
thin, long stems
curved, wavy, folded petals
butterfly floating near the flowers
all flowers have red and white
calm and tranquil, waving in the wind
I love the 'Chinese Garden' painting by Wong.

Dominic Wilkins (9)
East Court School for Dyslexia

Zombie Kennings

Graveyard haunter
Human killer
Blood sucker
Brain eater
Death bringer
Fear striker
Head splitter
Blood letter
Body halver
Flesh carver
Mercy killer.

Danny Griggs (10)
Edenbridge Primary School

Spooky - Haikus

In a dark basement
lives a demented hunchback
who eats bony soup

The corpse in the ground
who eats all human beings
soon will rise again

In a ghostly ship
there is a creepy spirit
who is bloodthirsty.

Emma James (11)
Edenbridge Primary School

Vampire Kennings

Eerie explorer
Vampire leader
One-eyed cruiser
Blood sucker
Creepy crawler
Spirit stealer
Underworld destroyer
High flyer
Dirty dancer
Dungeon liver
Graveyard haunter
Head splitter
Heart stopper.

James Bradford (10)
Edenbridge Primary School

Spiderwebs - Haiku

Spooky spiderwebs,
Silvery, sparkling webs shine
Dewdrops caught in webs.

Amber Chatten (11)
Edenbridge Primary School

Ghoul Kennings

Bone chiller
Ghoul stalker
Blood drinker
Child stealer
Human drainer
Spooky flyer
Inside sucker.

Chelsea Broadbery (11)
Edenbridge Primary School

Ghosts Of The Dead - Haiku

Ghosts and spirits scream,
Scaring little kids away,
Zombies will arise.

Lauren Nazer (10)
Edenbridge Primary School

Class Plant

We have a plant in class,
Everybody's had a glance,
But all you can see is bare soil.
It needs to have a chance.

There's a big seed that grows in soil,
It looks grand and royal,
It is the biggest seed in the world.
It's quite curled.

I put it in a pot on the floor next to the door,
I was sure no one would knock it.
I waited for days,
Finally a stalk came out,
I gave a shout.

I waited for the flower,
I waited for many an hour,
Then a flower came out.
I loved it.
I kissed it once
And then again, the class had a glance.

Isabel Cole (8)
Egerton CE Primary School

Runner Beans

Runner beans running up a pole
Running to the top
Out from the stalk
A little flower pops

Runner beans in the pan
Then they start to flutter
When they come out of the pan
That is when my tummy mutters

Runner beans are scrummy
Nestling in my tummy.

Emmanuel Ephenus-Agostinho (8)
Egerton CE Primary School

Growing Hops

I put a plant into the ground
And there appeared three shoots.
They twisted and turned clockwise,
The only plant in the world.

They grew upwards towards the sun,
Then appeared soft round things
Like little pine cones.

I picked them all to make some beer,
I cut off the shoots
But they grew once more.

When they dried they were prickly,
They sliced into my hands.
But earlier they were soft and smooth.
Give a cheer, we've made some beer!

Alice Reed (8)
Egerton CE Primary School

Seed

This is my seed,
my seed is very small,
it will grow very tall,
it makes me happy
while I'm playing with my ball.

It looks like a trumpet,
but you can't really play it,
while my mum is having a cup of tea,
I can plant a sweet pea,
it will look very pretty,
a hiding place for Kitty.

Lily Pevy (8)
Egerton CE Primary School

In My Head

In my head I see . . .
A sea of fish,
Being chased by sharks,
Swimming into a crack in a wall.
The sharks are eating the unlucky ones left behind.

In my head I see . . .
A diver jump into the sea
And stab those sharks
And they *die!*
That's what I see in my head.

Bradley Cain (9)
Egerton CE Primary School

In A Chicken's Head

In a chicken's head
There is grain flowing all around
And eggs hatching
In the chicken shed.

Soft golden hay
Ready to go to sleep
Waiting for the next day to come.

But they think of the fox
Lurking outside
Waiting for them
To fall asleep
And then come in
And take them to its den.

Jack Stubbins (8)
Egerton CE Primary School

In Emily's Head

In Emily's head
A dream roams
Waiting to escape
I will tell you this dream
With a whisper in the trees

One beautiful day
On a sunny beach
The sun is shining
The clouds, cotton wool balls
Floating above.
In a painted blue sky
And snow for ice cream
The trees singing in the wind
A wonderful dream
Definitely to be told.

Emilia King (8)
Egerton CE Primary School

The Word Party

(Based on 'The Word Party', Macmillan 1999)

Happy words make me grin,
Rude words hurt me just like pins,
Small words are easily missed,
Long words duck down small,
Cool words strut straight and tall,
Code words are hard to understand,
Careless words fall from my hand,
Swear words make me flare,
Mysterious words with others share,
Words and words of every type,
Which of these would you like?

Alisha Hameed (9)
Egerton CE Primary School

In My Head

In my head . . .
I have a time machine
To take me forwards
And backwards in time.
I might go back in time
To when I was a baby
Or
Maybe I will go forward in time
To see what it will be like
To be a grown-up and
To have a job working with people
Or maybe, I will just stay as I am
Right *now!*

Michael Carty (8)
Egerton CE Primary School

In A Footballer's Head

In a footballer's head there is a goal
And the footballer wants to score -
To score five goals.
He wants to go to Arsenal
But doesn't want a red card and to get sent off.

Jake Hirvela (9)
Egerton CE Primary School

In My Mum's Head

A messy house -
It's such a disgrace!
An untidy room -
She nearly faints.
Getting a headache
Phone's ringing
It all happens at once!
The hope of a holiday is her dream -
Kids calling,
'Is dinner ready?'
'What's for tea?'
What would I do without her?
She's always there for me!
I think I'm in her head -
For she's in mine!

Lauren Fox (8)
Egerton CE Primary School

In My Head

Mmm! A mouse is nice!
Wonder what a shrew tastes like?
It could be nice
I want to go outside
Be normal, chase and climb
I'll eat this food
Can't go to waste

Finally I'm out
To climb a tree
And snooze, *zzzzzz*

Then I'll catch birds
Mmmmm!
                    Nice!

Rachel Pries (8)
Egerton CE Primary School

In A King's Head . . .

There is a moat and a bridge
An evil wicked witch
There is a green hill with red dots
For her evil plan
Knights will charge on horses made of candy
And carry chocolate swords.

Charlie Banks (8)
Egerton CE Primary School

In My Head

In my head I saw
A fountain full of chocolate
Calling me to come and eat it
But when I did
I went back in time
To Chocolate Land
Where the houses were made of chocolate
And chocolate people ruled
A world so tasty
I never wanted to leave
Or see anything else
In my head.

Harriet Heathcote (9)
Egerton CE Primary School

In My Head

In my head
I'm in a field with my brother and my dog,
With my cat following behind.
The sky washed down with blue,
And cotton wool balls float about in the sky as clouds.
The grass has just been cut,
I can smell it,
All nice and fresh.

Ahead of us
There is a chocolate river,
The trees are covered in sugar.
I can hear the birds singing in the trees.

I can see my brother playing with my dog.
The flowers are candy,
Waiting to be eaten.

Wait, no . . .
I'm out of it now . . .
But I can't wait to go back.

Emily Gawler (9)
Egerton CE Primary School

In My Head

In my head there's a chocolate fountain,
As deep as a swimming pool,
In my head there's a party,
I'm not inviting Patrick Darty!
Everyone is singing along,
We're all going to play ping-pong,
There's a huge chocolate cake.

Eliza Wallis (8)
Egerton CE Primary School

In My Head

In my head there is a dream -
a dream come true.
It's a dream about a lovely blue sky,
with a butterfly fluttering on a tree,
a little breeze.
In my head it's a lovely sunny, hot day,
I'm swimming
In my pool,
larking about,
playing games
and inviting friends to come round.
In my head
I am thinking about . . .
going outside
on the trampoline,
playing 'Crack the egg'.

Katie Mills (9)
Egerton CE Primary School

In My Head

In my head
I'm lying in the park eating ice cream,
on a hot summer's day,
with children playing in the grass,
and kids playing football,
toddlers shouting,
getting over-excited,
sitting on a swing,
sliding down the slide,
children playing hide-and-seek in the woods,
oh no, it has gone!
Maybe next time I will explore more,
I'm lying in the park.

Ella Moore (8)
Egerton CE Primary School

Seeds

It started off a seed in the ground
Then it grew up, round and round
The rain came down without a sound onto the ground
The seed burst out with a pop of joy
It swirled up high towards the sky
The colours of a rainbow, pink, purple and blue
Expressing joy to me and you.

Erin Blackford (7)
Egerton CE Primary School

Flower Seeds

My seeds start to grow
Whoosh! They shoot up like a rocket
Bang! Pop! They explode with the colours of the rainbow.
Blue, pink, yellow and green,
Wow! What a display!
The best you've ever seen.

Ella Woodcock (8)
Egerton CE Primary School

In A Footballer's Head

In a footballer's head there are people
And a goal
And there's a flag on a pole
And him scoring a great goal
And everyone cheering.

Bill Hutt (9)
Egerton CE Primary School

Inside My Head

Inside my head there's a dream,
About a bike on custard,
A skateboard on chocolate,
A metal trampoline,
A bone made out of jelly,
A sugar castle,
The sun a purple colour,
The moon as green as an emerald,
A cat as springy as a pogo stick,
A spring that doesn't bounce,
A cannon blowing fire like a firework.

That's what's in my head,
What's in yours?

Joshua Simpson (8)
Egerton CE Primary School

In Her Head . . .

She's worrying about her first football match,
If she's going to score,
She's glad it's Tuesday for netball practice.
She can't wait for tomorrow because she's going to the cinema,
Afterwards her friend is coming round.
She doesn't know what they are going to play,
She thinks they should go in the garden,
She's got her own little bit.
She thinking, (yes, my sister's going somewhere
That means we can go in her room and muck around.)
That's what's in her head.

Sasha Gomez (9)
Egerton CE Primary School

In My Head

In my head there is a bully,
Why does he hurt me
And why doesn't he say sorry?
I also wonder about my party,
How will it go?
Will everyone like it?
Hopefully they will!
I think about horse riding,
What will this horse be like?
I don't know,
But I'm really excited.
That's what's in my head.
What's in yours?

Amelia Simpson (8)
Egerton CE Primary School

In My Head

In my head
I have a dream
In my dream there is a world
In that world there is a country called England
In England there is Kent
In Kent there is Egerton
In Egerton there is a school
In that school are children
Those children are the best.

Alishia Mason (9)
Egerton CE Primary School

Thoughts

I was looking into the sky one day,
All my bad thoughts seemed to drift away.
The dreamy clouds went floating by,
It looked like my thoughts went into the sky.

Not a bad thought in my body,
I was in Wonderland,
The bright yellow sun, as bright as eyes,
The puffy clouds like candyfloss.

The clouds looked like hearts and diamonds,
I lay there with my head in the sky,
Until the sun set with a red and purple dye.
That was the sun saying goodbye.

Holly Plumb (10)
Elliott Park School

Music

M usic is lovely, it sounds beautiful.
U sing music means the world to me.
S ometimes music sounds horrible
I f you play it wrong.
C lassical music is nice but I like Pop Party better.

S ome people can play absolutely anything,
O r if you don't want to play, you can sing.
U nusual sounds,
N ot always nice.
D eafening noises,
S ometimes very annoying.

Grace Hale (9)
Elliott Park School

Jamaica

Jamaica is a beautiful country,
With its intensifying heat,
Lush forests,
Dyed blue, sparkling and warm shimmering seas.
Lots of people enjoy going to Jamaica,
It is a tourist attraction,
With lots of things to do,
Small rock pools and nice people,
A cool breeze running through your hair.
You can scuba dive and swim with the dolphins,
Lots of people playing beach cricket and football,
You can climb so high, it seems like forever,
I like Jamaica and you will too.

Toby Box (10)
Elliott Park School

The Old Lady

I am an old lady and I am proud to be
I eat lots of disgusting things like bees and bear meat
But I am not happy because I shrink and get wrinkles
But when I smile I still get dimples
My son will get married and have babies
And I will look back on all these stages
It's great being old.

Ellice Turner (9)
Elliott Park School

Mirror Carp

Last night I caught a mirror carp,
It weighed about two pounds,
When I took the hook out of its mouth
It never made a sound.
The mirrors on its skin shone brightly
In the murky water.
My dad caught one which weighed about ten pounds,
The one I caught might have been its daughter.
When my dad took the hook out of its mouth
It made a lot of sound.
After that he caught a roach
Which only had one eye.
When we packed our stuff away
I shouted out *'Goodbye!'*

Harry Pierpoint (11)
Elliott Park School

The Wonder Of TV

Children like me
Always watch TV
They sit on the sofa eating sweets
Watching recipe programmes for baking treats

Some programmes are about going on holiday
And sunny days on beaches
Others are scary
And some have lots of pretty pink fairies

On TV we can learn about kings and queens
Wars, castles and flying machines
We can learn about badgers and lions that are wild
And even learn how to look after a child

There are programmes for adults and programmes for children
The programme titles range from A to Z
When it's time for the news at 10
That's when I will be in bed.

Siân Ayling (10)
Elliott Park School

My Best Friends

I always need a best friend,
To stick with me until the end,
When we begin to laugh,
We always get told off by the staff,
We share our secrets
And don't tell anyone who asks,
We always say, 'Best friends forever,'
We do our handshake,
And do our dance.
It's getting dark,
So we say goodbye,
And always say,
'Best friends forever.'

Tamara Layzell (11)
Elliott Park School

The Planets

There are so many planets I wonder why.
They are just hanging up in the sky.
We live on Earth, that is next to Mars,
Our planet is polluted because of cars.

On Venus they are at war, with Saturn,
We all want to know what is going to happen.
The sun shining bright, straight on the moon,
It is going to expand very, very soon.

Pluto is freezing, what a surprise!
Mercury is much bigger in size.
They are some planets but not all.
These are the ones I'm going to call.

Freddie Pierpoint (9)
Elliott Park School

Spring

Spring is when I play in the park
Because it is no longer dark.
The plants are growing up to the sky,
As all the new animals pass by.
All the colours in the light
Are a very beautiful sight.
We are playing in the mountainous grass
As all the colourful birds fly past.
Yes, spring is an excellent time
If we had to choose a season, this would be mine.

Matthew Edwards (10)
Elliott Park School

Fireworks

Fireworks are colourful
with wonderful sounds and bangs.
With the dark night at the back,
the sight of stars.
The bright stars up in the sky - the scent of light.
The fire burns to the end
with the smell of coal and matches.
Fireworks fly everywhere with the bonfire flames
climbing up in the air with black smoke.
You shake with the smell and see sparklers
flicking around on the ground.
The fire crackles all the time
and sticks turn to ash!

Tyler Pond-Field (11)
Elliott Park School

Pirates

Pirates fight
Fight like men
Sail dangerous seas
Sail through rocks
And through rough seas

They have gold
Hide it in caves
And carry rum
Drink all day and night

Skull and crossbones
Is the flag
Boats made of wood
Sink quickly

Cannons fire
Cannon balls fly
Very, very fast

Guns are dangerous
And very loud
Captains have an eye patch
And a wooden leg
And sometimes die.

Bertie Francis (9)
Elliott Park School

Spring

Bunny rabbits hopping,
Little lambs leaping,
Pretty flowers blooming,
Summer days longer,
Baby pigs being born,
Some rainy days to cool off,
Having fun days on the beach,
Climbing up trees in the garden.

Lacey Pavitt (9)
Elliott Park School

I Am A Duck

I am a duck, my name is Buck,
I play in the sun, having a lot of fun,
I live in this pond at the top of a hill,
Sometimes a man comes, his name is Bill,
He feeds me bread and pats my head,
I understand each word he says,
'Fly away, birdie, fly away!'
Unfortunately, I can only reply with a 'Quack'!
So Bill, he turns his back,
'Come back, come back!' I quack away,
Only hoping that he will stay.

Billie Cook (11)
Elliott Park School

Who Are You?

At the dark of the night,
At the end of the day,
Something came here
And it wouldn't go away.

In the hotel,
On the third floor,
Behind a wooden door,
A boy was asleep,
Then he heard a bird cheep.

The boy awoke,
As the thing spoke.
It was a bloke,
Wearing a cloak.

He had a knife,
And a picture of his wife.
He stuck it through,
It's quarter past two.

The birds flew in
Making a din,
Surrounding him.

He had escaped,
Man in a cape.

The boy hit his head
Fell into bed,
He felt the pain,
He was driven insane.

The witnesses thought they saw
A man walking a boar.
It must be his pet
He'd won in a bet.
The question roamed through,
'Who are you?'

Karl Edwards (11)
Hersden Community Primary School

Him

Knock upon the wooden door,
Of the Queen's Inn.
Stares out along the shore,
No home for him.
Making himself very clear,
He wants a dark room.
Just one starry night,
Hiding from the moon.
Slinging his bag,
He lies on the bed.
This is not a good place,
Just left with his head.
A grim frown,
Black tired eyes,
Crooked red nose,
And heart where it lies.
Stayed up all night,
His true colours shown.
Is he fat? Is he slim?
He is neither, just bone.
His cloak is hanging,
On his rough, bare skull.
Unprotected heart banging,
As his thoughts roll.

Ayesha Harris (10)
Hersden Community Primary School

Silence

S ilence is not loud
I t is cosy
L ovely and quiet
E njoyable
N icer than loud
C ooler than cheese
E nding silence is not cool.

William Ruse (8)
John Mayne CE Primary School

Silence

S ilence is in a boat on the river
I 'm in a box of silence
L et's be silent like the sea
E nter the box of silence
N o talking, we're in our box of silence
C an we be silent?
E nter through sign language.

Mark Sainsbury (8)
John Mayne CE Primary School

Silence

Silence is a lovely word, I really like it.
It makes me close my eyes at night-time.
It is so silent. I can't hear a word.
The word silence is beautiful.
It makes me not listen to anyone.
When you hear the wind blow
It is so, so silent.

Amber-Rose Lockwood (7)
John Mayne CE Primary School

Speak

Talk can be quiet
Talk can be loud
Talk is shouting
Talk is laughing
Talk is humming
Talk is praying to God
It can be loud or not
Whispering to a person is still talking!

Sam Hackney (8)
John Mayne CE Primary School

Silence

S ilence is quiet
I t is soundless
L ovely!
E very day silence is lovely
N othing
C osy
E nter the silence.

Elliot Steward (8)
John Mayne CE Primary School

Long Beard Lobster

Down in the ocean on the seabed
There is a lobster
With a beard thicker than a woolly jumper
The biggest in the world
Also . . .
His head is as colossal as a massive whale
His eyes are as small as a tiny pea
His feet are as big as an angry giant stomping along the floor
But . . .
His body is as shiny as a sparkling diamond
His whiskers are as red as a flaming-hot sun
His skin is as scaly as a terrifying fish
With a tail as hairy as *King Kong.*

Jed Morgans (9)
John Mayne CE Primary School

My School Life

What I love about school is
The enjoyment of the lessons,
And the generous help of the teachers.

What I hate about *teachers* is
Their evil look,
To them chaining you in at break.

What I love about break is
The games we play,
And the skipping rope games.

What I hate about games is
When the boys play 'Girls vs Boys' chase,
Running ragged around in circles then time to go to assembly.

What I love about assembly is
The quiet room and a peaceful voice no one can hear,
Singing calm songs and hearing soft voices,
Then going back to the classroom.

What I hate about the classroom is
The high-pitched noise and chaos,
People pushing and shoving.

What I love about school is
The enjoyment of the lessons,
And the generous help of the teachers.

Holly Palliser (9)
John Mayne CE Primary School

My Bedroom Window

In the summer I can see,
Cows are grazing by the tree,
The field looks like a sea of green,
It's a quiet and peaceful scene.

In the winter the trees go white,
And the temperature falls from a great height,
Then slowly the grass dies,
What a shock to my eyes!

In the autumn leaves drift down,
And they cover the whole town,
Then the squirrel gets its food,
That puts me into a quiet mood.

In the spring the leaves grow,
And the grass - *wow!*
Now the baby lambs are born,
And farmers start growing the corn.

Thomas Agu Benson (8)
John Mayne CE Primary School

Puffle

Deep in the ocean at the bottom of the sea is . . .
A creature that you'd never believe!
A small little fur ball snuggled right up
In a cosy bed of glittering grass.
Her eyes are balmy
And as kind as a puppy's.
She is as fuzzy as a bear
And as warm as a red-hot fire.
Her fur is as pink as roses
And as shiny as pale pink crystals . . .
And her name is Puffle.
She jumps and plays in the ocean all day,
But beware . . .
She can turn you into a statue of the sea,
If you look into those eyes.

Emily Ruse (9)
John Mayne CE Primary School

Young Writers Information

We hope you have enjoyed reading this book - and that you will continue to enjoy it in the coming years.

If you like reading and writing poetry drop us a line, or give us a call, and we'll send you a free information pack.

Alternatively if you would like to order further copies of this book or any of our other titles, then please give us a call or log onto our website at www.youngwriters.co.uk

**Young Writers Information
Remus House
Coltsfoot Drive
Peterborough
PE2 9JX**

(01733) 890066